TABLE OF CONTENT

Mask 16: Vengeful

Mask 17: Abusive

Mask 18: Deeply flawed

Mask 19: Prejudiced

Mask 20: Narcissists

INTRODUCTION

We all wear masks in our lives. Sometimes these masks serve as protection from the harsh realities of the world around us. Other times, they allow us to present a version of ourselves that we believe is more acceptable or likeable to others. But what happens when these masks become our true identities? What happens when we become so entrenched in the personas we have created that we can no longer distinguish between who we are and who we pretend to be?

In "The Masks We Wear," we explore the various masks that people wear in their daily lives. We delve into the traits that define these masks, the impact they have on both the wearer and those around them, and provide practical advice on how to identify and avoid them.

Each chapter of this book focuses on a specific mask, such as the unfaithful partner, the manipulative coworker, or the narcissist. We examine the underlying fears and insecurities that drive individuals to create these false identities, and the toll it takes on their relationships and their own sense of self.

We then provide guidance on how to identify when someone is wearing one of these masks, such as recognizing patterns of behaviour or paying attention to red flags. We also offer practical strategies on how to avoid these individuals or limit their impact on our lives, such as setting boundaries or seeking support from others.

Ultimately, "The Masks We Wear" is a powerful exploration of the human experience, and a reminder that beneath the masks we wear, we are all deeply flawed and complex individuals striving to find our place in the world.

UNFAITHFUL

Unfaithful people are individuals who engage in behaviour that violates the expectations or agreements of a committed relationship. This can include engaging in sexual or emotional relationships with people outside of the committed relationship, lying about one's actions or whereabouts, or withholding intimacy or emotional connection from one's partner.

How to Recognize Unfaithful People:

Recognizing unfaithful people can be difficult, as some individuals may hide their behaviour or exhibit subtle signs. However, there are some common signs to look for, such as:

Changes in behaviour or routine: Unfaithful people may suddenly become more secretive about their activities or whereabouts, or may make excuses for why they can't spend time with their partner.

Emotional distance: They may become emotionally distant from their partner, or may seem uninterested in engaging in physical or emotional intimacy.

Lying or being evasive: Unfaithful people may be dishonest or evasive when asked direct questions about their behaviour or whereabouts.

Increased interest in appearance or self-care: Unfaithful people may suddenly become more concerned with their appearance, grooming habits, or physical fitness.

How to Avoid Unfaithful People:

Avoiding unfaithful people may be necessary if you wish to protect yourself from potential emotional pain and turmoil. Some strategies for avoiding unfaithful people include:

Trust your instincts: If something feels off in your relationship or you suspect that your partner may be engaging in unfaithful behaviour, it's important to trust your instincts and communicate your concerns.

Set clear expectations: Establishing clear expectations and boundaries with your partner can help prevent unfaithful behaviour. Make sure to communicate your needs and values and work together to establish a strong foundation of trust and honesty.

Seek support: If you are struggling with the aftermath of unfaithful behaviour, it's important to seek support from trusted friends, family members, or a therapist.

Take care of yourself: Taking care of yourself is crucial when dealing with unfaithful behaviour. Make sure to prioritize your own needs and practice self-care activities that help you feel grounded and centred.

Ultimately, avoiding unfaithful people may involve making difficult decisions about your relationships and priorities. It's important to remember that you deserve to be treated with respect and honesty in all of your relationships.

MANIPULATIVE

Manipulative people are individuals who use tactics such as deceit, flattery, or coercion to control or influence others. They may exploit others for personal gain or seek to gain power or advantage in relationships or situations.

How to Recognize Manipulative People:

Recognizing manipulative people can be challenging, as they may hide their true intentions or use subtle tactics to influence others. However, there are some signs to look for, such as:

Flattery or charm: Manipulative people may use flattery or charm to gain trust or favour.

Controlling behaviour: They may try to control the actions or decisions of others or may become angry or defensive when their authority is questioned.

Lack of empathy: Manipulative people may be unwilling or unable to empathize with others or to understand their perspectives.

Unreliable or inconsistent behaviour: They may make promises or commitments that they do not follow through on, or may change their opinions or values to suit their needs.

How to Avoid Manipulative People:

Avoiding manipulative people can be challenging, as they may be skilled at hiding their true nature. However, there are some strategies that you can use to limit their impact on your life, such as:

Trust your instincts: If something feels off in a relationship or situation, it's important to trust your instincts and take steps to protect yourself.

Establish clear boundaries: Setting clear boundaries with manipulative people can help prevent them from exploiting or controlling you. Make sure to communicate your needs and values and work to establish a foundation of trust and mutual respect.

Seek support: If you are struggling to deal with a manipulative person, it can be helpful to seek support from trusted friends, family members, or a therapist.

Practice self-care: Taking care of yourself is crucial when dealing with manipulative people. Make sure to prioritize your own needs and engage in activities that help you feel grounded and centred.

Ultimately, avoiding manipulative people may involve making difficult decisions about your relationships or situations. It's important to remember that you deserve to be treated with respect and fairness and that you have the power to set boundaries and protect yourself from harmful behaviour.

DECEITFUL

Deceitful people are individuals who engage in behaviour that involves lying, deceiving, or misleading others. They may use deception to gain personal advantage or to avoid negative consequences.

How to Recognize Deceitful People:

Recognizing deceitful people can be challenging, as they may be skilled at hiding their true intentions or behaviour. However, there are some signs to look for, such as:

Inconsistencies in their story: Deceitful people may struggle to keep their lies straight, leading to inconsistencies in their stories.

Avoiding eye contact: They may avoid making eye contact or appear nervous or uncomfortable when asked direct questions.

Contradicting behaviour: Deceitful people may behave in ways that contradict their words or intentions.

Withholding information: They may withhold important details or information that could contradict their story or reveal their true intentions.

How to Avoid Deceitful People:

Avoiding deceitful people can be challenging, as they may be skilled at hiding their true nature. However, there are some strategies that you can use to limit their impact on your life, such as:

Trust your instincts: If something feels off in a relationship or situation, it's important to trust your instincts and take steps to protect yourself.

Verify information: It's important to verify information that you receive from others in order to ensure that it is accurate and truthful.

Be cautious with personal information: Deceitful people may use personal information against you, so it's important to be cautious about what information you share.

Seek support: If you are struggling to deal with a deceitful person, it can be helpful to seek support from trusted friends, family members, or a therapist.

Ultimately, avoiding deceitful people may involve making difficult decisions about your relationships or situations. It's important to remember that you deserve to be treated with respect and honesty and that you have the power to protect yourself from harmful behaviour.

SELFISH

Selfish people are individuals who prioritize their own needs and desires above those of others, often at the expense of others. They may lack empathy for others and may be unwilling to make sacrifices or compromises in order to benefit others.

How to Recognize Selfish People:

Recognizing selfish people can be challenging, as they may be skilled at hiding their true intentions or behaviour. However, there are some signs to look for, such as:

Lack of consideration for others: Selfish people may be dismissive of the needs or feelings of others, or may prioritize their own needs above those of others.

Lack of empathy: They may be unwilling or unable to understand or empathize with the needs and feelings of others.

Refusal to compromise: Selfish people may be unwilling to make compromises or sacrifices in order to benefit others.

Arrogance or entitlement: They may have an inflated sense of self-importance or entitlement, or may believe that they are inherently more deserving than others.

How to Avoid Selfish People:

Avoiding selfish people can be challenging, as they may be skilled at hiding their true nature. However, there are some strategies that you can use to limit their impact on your life, such as:

Set clear boundaries: It's important to establish clear boundaries with selfish people and to communicate your needs and expectations.

Avoid enabling their behaviour: It's important not to enable selfish behaviour by allowing them to take advantage of you or others.

Focus on healthy relationships: Prioritize relationships with people who share your values and who prioritize mutual respect and empathy.

Practice self-care: Taking care of yourself is crucial when dealing with selfish people. Make sure to prioritize your own needs and engage in activities that help you feel grounded and centred.

Ultimately, avoiding selfish people may involve making difficult decisions about your relationships or situations. It's important to remember that you deserve to be treated with respect and fairness and that you have the power to set boundaries and protect yourself from harmful behaviour.

DISHONEST

Dishonest people are individuals who engage in behaviour that involves lying, cheating, or deceiving others. They may present false information or withhold important details in order to manipulate or mislead others.

How to Recognize Dishonest People:

Recognizing dishonest people can be challenging, as they may be skilled at hiding their true intentions or behaviour. However, there are some signs to look for, such as:

Inconsistencies in their story: Dishonest people may struggle to keep their lies straight, leading to inconsistencies in their stories.

Lack of transparency: They may be unwilling or unable to provide clear or complete information about their actions or intentions.

Unreliable or inconsistent behaviour: Dishonest people may make promises or commitments that they do not follow through on, or may change their opinions or values to suit their needs.

Lack of accountability: They may be unwilling to take responsibility for their actions or to admit when they have made a mistake.

How to Avoid Dishonest People:

Avoiding dishonest people can be challenging, as they may be skilled at hiding their true nature. However, there are some strategies that you can use to limit their impact on your life, such

as:

Verify information: It's important to verify information that you receive from others in order to ensure that it is accurate and truthful.

Watch for red flags: Pay attention to inconsistencies in their story or behaviour, and be wary of anyone who seems reluctant to provide clear or complete information.

Set clear expectations: It's important to communicate your expectations and values clearly, and to establish a foundation of trust and mutual respect.

Seek support: If you are struggling to deal with a dishonest person, it can be helpful to seek support from trusted friends, family members, or a therapist.

Ultimately, avoiding dishonest people may involve making difficult decisions about your relationships or situations. It's important to remember that you deserve to be treated with honesty and integrity and that you have the power to protect yourself from harmful behaviour.

CLOSED-MINDED

Closed-minded people are individuals who are unwilling or unable to consider new or different ideas, perspectives, or experiences. They may be rigid in their beliefs and resistant to change or growth.

How to Recognize Closed-minded People:

Recognizing closed-minded people can be challenging, as they may not always exhibit overtly negative behaviour. However, there are some signs to look for, such as:

Inflexibility: Closed-minded people may be inflexible in their beliefs or behaviour, and may resist change or growth.

Narrow-mindedness: They may have a narrow view of the world or be unwilling to consider alternative perspectives or experiences.

Judgmental behaviour: Closed-minded people may be quick to judge or criticize others who have different beliefs or experiences.

Lack of curiosity: They may lack curiosity about new or different ideas, and may be unwilling to engage in open-minded discussion or exploration.

How to Avoid Closed-minded People:

Avoiding closed-minded people can be challenging, as they may be a part of your social circle or workplace. However, there are some strategies that you can use to limit their impact on your life, such as:

Seek out open-minded individuals: Prioritize relationships with people who are open to new ideas and perspectives, and who engage in thoughtful discussion and exploration.

Challenge your own beliefs: It's important to challenge your own beliefs and perspectives in order to stay open-minded and avoid becoming closed off to new ideas.

Avoid getting into arguments: Closed-minded people may be unwilling to engage in open-minded discussion or exploration, so it's important to avoid getting into arguments or confrontations.

Focus on personal growth: Prioritize your own personal growth and development, and engage in activities that encourage open-mindedness and exploration.

Ultimately, avoiding closed-minded people may involve making difficult decisions about your relationships or situations. It's important to remember that you deserve to be surrounded by people who encourage growth and exploration and that you have the power to set boundaries and protect yourself from harmful behaviour.

JUDGEMENTAL

Judgmental people are individuals who are quick to form negative opinions or make critical judgments about others, often based on limited or incomplete information. They may be overly critical or harsh in their assessments and may be unwilling to consider different perspectives or experiences.

How to Recognize Judgmental People:

Recognizing judgmental people can be challenging, as they may not always exhibit overtly negative behaviour. However, there are some signs to look for, such as:

Criticizing others: Judgmental people may be quick to criticize or judge others, often based on limited or incomplete information.

Being dismissive: They may be dismissive of other people's experiences or perspectives and may be unwilling to engage in open-minded discussion or exploration.

Using negative language: Judgmental people may use negative or harsh language when talking about others and may focus on flaws or shortcomings rather than strengths or positive qualities.

Being closed-minded: They may be unwilling to consider different perspectives or experiences and may cling to their own beliefs or opinions.

How to Avoid Judgmental People:

Avoiding judgmental people can be challenging, as they may be a

part of your social circle or workplace. However, there are some strategies that you can use to limit their impact on your life, such as:

Prioritize relationships with positive people: Seek out relationships with people who focus on strengths and positive qualities, and who are open to different perspectives and experiences.

Challenge your own assumptions: It's important to challenge your own assumptions and biases in order to avoid becoming judgmental.

Set boundaries: If you are dealing with a judgmental person, it's important to set clear boundaries and communicate your needs and expectations.

Practice self-care: Taking care of yourself is crucial when dealing with judgmental people. Make sure to prioritize your own needs and engage in activities that help you feel grounded and centred.

Ultimately, avoiding judgmental people may involve making difficult decisions about your relationships or situations. It's important to remember that you deserve to be treated with respect and understanding and that you have the power to set boundaries and protect yourself from harmful behaviour.

ENVIOUS AND JEALOUS

Envious and jealous people are individuals who feel resentful or bitter towards others who possess something that they do not have, whether it is material possessions, achievements, or relationships. They may experience feelings of inadequacy or insecurity and may react with hostility or negativity towards those who they perceive as threats.

How to Recognize Envious and Jealous People:

Recognizing envious and jealous people can be challenging, as they may not always exhibit overtly negative behaviour. However, there are some signs to look for, such as:

Resentment towards others' success: Envious and jealous people may express resentment or bitterness towards others who achieve success or attain material possessions.

Engaging in competitive behaviour: They may engage in competitive behaviour, either openly or covertly, in order to prove their worth or to outdo others.

Sabotaging behaviour: Envious and jealous people may engage in behaviour designed to undermine or sabotage others' success or happiness.

Constantly comparing themselves to others: They may constantly compare themselves to others, leading to feelings of inadequacy or insecurity.

How to Avoid Envious and Jealous People:

Avoiding envious and jealous people can be challenging, as they may be a part of your social circle or workplace. However, there are some strategies that you can use to limit their impact on your life, such as:

Avoid engaging in competition: It's important to avoid engaging in competitive behaviour with envious and jealous people, as this may only fuel their negative emotions.

Focus on your own achievements: Instead of comparing yourself to others, focus on your own achievements and accomplishments.

Set boundaries: If you are dealing with an envious or jealous person, it's important to set clear boundaries and communicate your needs and expectations.

Seek support: If you are struggling to deal with an envious or jealous person, seek support from trusted friends, family members, or a therapist.

Ultimately, avoiding envious and jealous people may involve making difficult decisions about your relationships or situations. It's important to remember that you deserve to be celebrated for your achievements and to be surrounded by people who support and uplift you and that you have the power to set boundaries and protect yourself from harmful behaviour.

PETTY

Petty people are individuals who hold onto feelings of anger, resentment, or bitterness towards others, often over minor or insignificant issues. They may be unwilling or unable to let go of past grievances and may engage in behaviour designed to seek revenge or punishment.

How to Recognize Petty People:

Recognizing petty people can be challenging, as they may not always exhibit overtly negative behaviour. However, there are some signs to look for, such as:

Holding onto past grievances: Petty people may bring up past issues or events repeatedly, even when they are not relevant to the current situation.

Being overly sensitive: They may react strongly to even minor criticism or perceived slights and may take things personally.

Engaging in passive-aggressive behaviour: Petty people may engage in passive-aggressive behaviour, such as making snide comments or withholding information.

Refusing to let go: They may be unwilling or unable to let go of past grievances and may hold onto grudges for long periods of time.

How to Avoid Petty People:

Avoiding petty people can be challenging, as they may be a part of your social circle or workplace. However, there are some strategies that you can use to limit their impact on your life, such as:

Address issues directly: If you are dealing with a petty or hold grudges person, it's important to address any issues or grievances directly and respectfully.

Set boundaries: It's important to set clear boundaries and communicate your needs and expectations with a petty or hold grudges person.

Avoid engaging in negative behaviour: Refrain from engaging in negative behaviour, such as gossiping or spreading rumours, as this may only fuel their negative emotions.

Seek support: If you are struggling to deal with a petty or hold grudges person, seek support from trusted friends, family members, or a therapist.

Ultimately, avoiding petty people may involve making difficult decisions about your relationships or situations. It's important to remember that you deserve to be surrounded by people who are willing to work through issues and move forward in a positive and respectful manner and that you have the power to set boundaries and protect yourself from harmful behaviour.

PASSIVE-AGGRESSIVE

Passive-aggressive people are individuals who express their negative feelings in an indirect or passive manner, rather than addressing them directly. They may use sarcasm, backhanded compliments, or other subtle behaviours to express their displeasure or frustration.

How to Recognize Passive-Aggressive People:

Recognizing passive-aggressive people can be challenging, as they may not always exhibit overtly negative behaviour. However, there are some signs to look for, such as:

Sulking or giving silent treatment: Passive-aggressive people may withdraw and refuse to communicate when they are upset or displeased.

Using sarcasm or backhanded compliments: They may use sarcasm or backhanded compliments to express their negative feelings towards others.

Being unresponsive or uncooperative: Passive-aggressive people may be unresponsive or uncooperative when asked to do something, as a way of expressing their displeasure.

Procrastinating or being intentionally inefficient: They may procrastinate or intentionally be inefficient in their work as a way of expressing their negative feelings.

How to Avoid Passive-Aggressive People:

Avoiding passive-aggressive people can be challenging, as they may be a part of your social circle or workplace. However, there are some strategies that you can use to limit their impact on your life, such as:

Address issues directly: If you are dealing with a passive-aggressive person, it's important to address any issues or grievances directly and respectfully.

Set boundaries: It's important to set clear boundaries and communicate your needs and expectations with a passive-aggressive person.

Avoid engaging in negative behaviour: Refrain from engaging in negative behaviour, such as gossiping or spreading rumours, as this may only fuel their negative emotions.

Seek support: If you are struggling to deal with a passive-aggressive person, seek support from trusted friends, family members, or a therapist.

Ultimately, avoiding passive-aggressive people may involve making difficult decisions about your relationships or situations. It's important to remember that you deserve to be surrounded by people who are willing to communicate openly and directly and that you have the power to set boundaries and protect yourself from harmful behaviour.

HYPOCRITE

Hypocrite people are individuals who act in a way that is inconsistent with their beliefs, values, or principles. They may hold others to a higher standard than they hold themselves, or they may preach one thing but practice another.

How to Recognize Hypocrite People:

Recognizing hypocritical people can be challenging, as they may not always exhibit overtly negative behaviour. However, there are some signs to look for, such as:

Saying one thing and doing another: Hypocrite people may say one thing but do the opposite, or they may hold others to a standard that they themselves do not follow.

Presenting a false image: They may present a false image of themselves to others, pretending to be someone they are not.

Blaming others for their own shortcomings: Hypocrite people may blame others for their own shortcomings, rather than take responsibility for their actions.

Making excuses for their behaviour: They may make excuses for their behaviour or try to justify it, even when it is inconsistent with their beliefs or values.

How to Avoid Hypocrite People:

Avoiding hypocritical people can be challenging, as they may be a part of your social circle or workplace. However, there are some strategies that you can use to limit their impact on your life, such

as:

Pay attention to actions, not just words: It's important to pay attention to people's actions, not just their words, in order to determine if they are being consistent with their beliefs and values.

Be wary of false images: It's important to be wary of people who present false images of themselves to others and to take the time to get to know them better.

Hold them accountable: If you are dealing with a hypocritical person, it's important to hold them accountable for their actions and to call them out on any inconsistencies or double standards.

Seek support: If you are struggling to deal with a hypocritical person, seek support from trusted friends, family members, or a therapist.

Ultimately, avoiding hypocritical people may involve making difficult decisions about your relationships or situations. It's important to remember that you deserve to be surrounded by people who are honest and consistent in their beliefs and values and that you have the power to set boundaries and protect yourself from harmful behaviour.

INTOLERANT

I ntolerant people are individuals who are unwilling or unable to accept the beliefs, opinions, or lifestyles of others. They may be dismissive or hostile towards those who hold different views or values and may refuse to engage in meaningful dialogue or compromise.

How to Recognize Intolerant People:

Recognizing intolerant people can be challenging, as they may not always exhibit overtly negative behaviour. However, there are some signs to look for, such as:

Being dismissive of others' views: Intolerant people may be dismissive or condescending towards those who hold different beliefs or opinions.

Refusing to engage in dialogue: They may refuse to engage in meaningful dialogue or compromise, insisting that their own views are the only valid ones.

Acting hostile or aggressive: Intolerant people may act hostile or aggressive towards those who hold different views or lifestyles.

Stereotyping or labelling others: They may stereotype or label others based on their beliefs or lifestyles, rather than taking the time to understand them as individuals.

How to Avoid Intolerant People:

Avoiding intolerant people can be challenging, as they may be a

part of your social circle or workplace. However, there are some strategies that you can use to limit their impact on your life, such as:

Set boundaries: It's important to set clear boundaries and communicate your needs and expectations with intolerant people.

Avoid engaging in negative behaviour: Refrain from engaging in negative behaviour, such as gossiping or spreading rumours, as this may only fuel their negative emotions.

Seek out like-minded individuals: Seek out like-minded individuals who share your beliefs and values, and who are open to meaningful dialogue and compromise.

Educate yourself: Educate yourself on different beliefs, opinions, and lifestyles in order to broaden your own understanding and tolerance.

Ultimately, avoiding intolerant people may involve making difficult decisions about your relationships or situations. It's important to remember that you deserve to be surrounded by people who are willing to engage in respectful dialogue and who value diversity and understanding and that you have the power to set boundaries and protect yourself from harmful behaviour.

ENTITLED

Entitled people are individuals who believe that they are deserving of special privileges or treatment, often without putting in the effort or work required to earn them. They may feel that they are owed something simply because of who they are or what they have achieved.

How to Recognize Entitled People:

Recognizing entitled people can be challenging, as they may not always exhibit overtly negative behaviour. However, there are some signs to look for, such as:

Believing that rules don't apply to them: Entitled people may feel that rules or expectations don't apply to them, or that they are above them.

Demanding special treatment or privileges: They may demand special treatment or privileges without putting in the effort or work required to earn them.

Acting entitled or arrogant: Entitled people may act entitled or arrogant towards others, believing that they are superior or more important.

Refusing to take responsibility for their actions: They may refuse to take responsibility for their actions, instead blaming others or external circumstances for their failures or mistakes.

How to Avoid Entitled People:

Avoiding entitled people can be challenging, as they may be a part of your social circle or workplace. However, there are some strategies that you can use to limit their impact on your life, such as:

Set boundaries: It's important to set clear boundaries and communicate your needs and expectations with entitled people.

Avoid enabling behaviour: Refrain from enabling entitled behaviour, such as giving in to demands or making excuses for their actions.

Focus on your own goals and achievements: Instead of comparing yourself to entitled people or feeling resentful of their privilege, focus on your own goals and achievements.

Seek support: If you are struggling to deal with an entitled person, seek support from trusted friends, family members, or a therapist.

Ultimately, avoiding entitled people may involve making difficult decisions about your relationships or situations. It's important to remember that you deserve to be surrounded by people who are willing to work hard and earn their achievements and that you have the power to set boundaries and protect yourself from harmful behaviour.

UNGRATEFUL

U ngrateful people are individuals who fail to appreciate the kindness, help, or generosity of others. They may take others for granted, and may not show appreciation or gratitude for the efforts or sacrifices made on their behalf.

How to Recognize Ungrateful People:

Recognizing ungrateful people can be challenging, as they may not always exhibit overtly negative behaviour. However, there are some signs to look for, such as:

Failing to say "thank you": Ungrateful people may fail to say "thank you" or show appreciation for kind gestures, gifts, or acts of service.

Taking others for granted: They may take others for granted, assuming that they will always be there to help or support them.

Criticizing or complaining: Ungrateful people may criticize or complain about the efforts or sacrifices made on their behalf, rather than showing gratitude or appreciation.

Feeling entitled: They may feel entitled to the help or support of others, without acknowledging the effort or sacrifice involved.

How to Avoid Ungrateful People:

Avoiding ungrateful people can be challenging, as they may be a part of your social circle or workplace. However, there are some strategies that you can use to limit their impact on your life, such

as:

Set boundaries: It's important to set clear boundaries and communicate your needs and expectations with ungrateful people.

Express your needs and feelings: Let them know how their ungrateful behaviour makes you feel and express your need for appreciation and gratitude.

Refocus your efforts: Instead of continuing to give to ungrateful people, refocus your efforts on those who are willing to appreciate and reciprocate your kindness.

Practice gratitude: Focus on expressing gratitude for the people and things in your own life, and surround yourself with those who also practice gratitude.

Ultimately, avoiding ungrateful people may involve making difficult decisions about your relationships or situations. It's important to remember that you deserve to be appreciated and valued and that you have the power to set boundaries and protect yourself from harmful behaviour.

TWO-FACED

Two-faced people are individuals who behave in one way to your face but speak or act differently behind your back. They may be insincere, dishonest, or manipulative, and may use their charm to gain your trust before betraying it.

How to Recognize Two-Faced People:

Recognizing two-faced people can be challenging, as they may be skilled at hiding their true intentions. However, there are some signs to look for, such as:

Inconsistencies in their behaviour: Two-faced people may act differently when you're not around, or may say one thing to your face and another behind your back.

Gossip or rumours: If you hear rumours or gossip about yourself or others, it may be a sign that someone is two-faced.

Insincere compliments or flattery: Two-faced people may use insincere compliments or flattery to manipulate you.

Trust your intuition: If you have a gut feeling that something isn't right, it's important to trust your instincts and investigate further.

How to Avoid Two-Faced People:

Avoiding two-faced people can be challenging, as they may be a part of your social circle or workplace. However, there are some strategies that you can use to limit their impact on your life, such

as:

Keep your distance: If possible, limit your interactions with two-faced people and avoid giving them personal information or access to your life.

Be cautious: Be cautious when dealing with new people and take the time to get to know them before trusting them.

Communicate openly: Communicate openly and honestly with those you trust, and seek their advice and support when dealing with two-faced people.

Stand up for yourself: If you are being targeted by a two-faced person, stand up for yourself and assert your boundaries.

Ultimately, avoiding two-faced people may involve making difficult decisions about your relationships or situations. It's important to remember that you deserve to be surrounded by people who are trustworthy and genuine and that you have the power to set boundaries and protect yourself from harmful behaviour.

VENGEFUL

Vengeful people are individuals who seek revenge or retaliation against those who they feel have wronged them. They may hold grudges, harbour resentment, and act out in harmful or destructive ways towards those they perceive as their enemies.

How to Recognize Vengeful People:

Recognizing vengeful people can be challenging, as they may be skilled at hiding their true intentions. However, there are some signs to look for, such as:

Focus on revenge: Vengeful people may talk frequently about seeking revenge or retaliation against those who have wronged them.

Holding grudges: They may hold grudges against others, even for minor offences, and refuse to let go of past hurts or slights.

Acting out in harmful or destructive ways: Vengeful people may act out in harmful or destructive ways towards those they perceive as their enemies.

Refusing to forgive or reconcile: They may refuse to forgive or reconcile with those who they perceive as their enemies, even if it would be in their best interest to do so.

How to Avoid Vengeful People:

Avoiding vengeful people can be challenging, as they may be a

part of your social circle or workplace. However, there are some strategies that you can use to limit their impact on your life, such as:

Keep your distance: If possible, limit your interactions with vengeful people and avoid giving them personal information or access to your life.

Do not engage: Refrain from engaging in arguments or conflicts with vengeful people, as this may escalate their behaviour.

Practice forgiveness: Focus on forgiving those who have wronged you, even if they do not seek forgiveness in return.

Seek support: If you are being targeted by a vengeful person, seek support from trusted friends, family members, or a therapist.

Ultimately, avoiding vengeful people may involve making difficult decisions about your relationships or situations. It's important to remember that you deserve to be surrounded by people who are willing to work towards reconciliation and forgiveness and that you have the power to set boundaries and protect yourself from harmful behaviour.

ABUSIVE

A busive people are individuals who use their power or control over others to inflict harm, whether physical, emotional, or psychological. They may use tactics such as intimidation, manipulation, and coercion to maintain their power and control over their victims.

How to Recognize Abusive People:

Recognizing abusive people can be challenging, as they may be skilled at hiding their true intentions. However, there are some signs to look for, such as:

Control: Abusive people may attempt to control every aspect of their victim's life, including finances, friendships, and daily activities.

Isolation: They may isolate their victim from friends and family members, making it difficult for the victim to seek help or support.

Intimidation: Abusive people may use intimidation tactics, such as threatening language or physical violence, to maintain their power and control.

Blaming: They may blame their victim for their own abusive behaviour, making it difficult for the victim to leave the relationship.

How to Avoid Abusive People:

Avoiding abusive people is essential for your safety and well-being. There are some strategies that you can use to limit their impact on your life, such as:

Seek help: If you are in an abusive situation, seek help from a trusted friend, family member, or professional.

Create a safety plan: Create a safety plan in case of an emergency, including identifying safe places to go and people to contact.

Set boundaries: Set clear boundaries with abusive people and communicate your expectations for how you should be treated.

Cut off contact: If possible, cut off contact with abusive people and seek a restraining order if necessary.

Ultimately, avoiding abusive people may involve making difficult decisions about your relationships or situations. It's important to remember that you deserve to be treated with respect and kindness and that you have the power to protect yourself from harmful behaviour.

DEEPLY FLAWED

Deeply flawed people are individuals who have significant character flaws or issues that may impact their ability to form healthy relationships and interact with others in a positive way. These flaws may manifest as problematic behaviour, emotional instability, or other negative traits.

How to Recognize Deeply Flawed People:

Recognizing deeply flawed people can be challenging, as they may be skilled at hiding their flaws. However, there are some signs to look for, such as:

Unpredictable behaviour: Deeply flawed people may have unpredictable or unstable behaviour, making it difficult to predict their actions or reactions.

A pattern of negative relationships: They may have a pattern of negative relationships, such as frequent arguments or breakups.

Lack of self-awareness: Deeply flawed people may lack self-awareness or insight into their own behaviour.

Difficulty with boundaries: They may struggle to respect boundaries or may have difficulty setting boundaries for themselves.

How to Avoid Deeply Flawed People:

Avoiding deeply flawed people can be challenging, as they may be a part of your social circle or workplace. However, there are some strategies that you can use to limit their impact on your life, such as:

Be cautious: Be cautious when dealing with new people and take the time to get to know them before investing emotionally.

Set boundaries: Set clear boundaries with deeply flawed people and communicate your expectations for how you should be treated.

Seek support: Seek support from trusted friends, family members, or a therapist if you are struggling to navigate a relationship with a deeply flawed person.

Practice self-care: Practice self-care and prioritize your own well-being when dealing with deeply flawed people.

Ultimately, avoiding deeply flawed people may involve making difficult decisions about your relationships or situations. It's important to remember that you deserve to be surrounded by people who are healthy and supportive and that you have the power to protect yourself from harmful behaviour.

PREJUDICED

P rejudiced people are individuals who hold negative attitudes or beliefs about individuals or groups based on their race, ethnicity, religion, gender, sexual orientation, or other characteristics. Prejudiced behaviour can take many forms, such as discrimination, stereotyping, or marginalizing individuals based on their group membership.

How to Recognize Prejudiced People:

Recognizing prejudiced people can be challenging, as they may not always express their attitudes or beliefs openly. However, there are some signs to look for, such as:

Negative stereotypes: Prejudiced people may hold negative stereotypes about individuals or groups based on their race, ethnicity, religion, gender, sexual orientation, or other characteristics.

Discriminatory behaviour: They may engage in discriminatory behaviour towards individuals or groups based on their group membership.

Marginalization: Prejudiced people may marginalize individuals or groups, making it difficult for them to access resources or participate fully in society.

Insensitive language: They may use insensitive language or slurs when referring to individuals or groups based on their group membership.

How to Avoid Prejudiced People:

Avoiding prejudiced people can be challenging, as they may be a part of your social circle or workplace. However, there are some strategies that you can use to limit their impact on your life, such as:

Set boundaries: Set clear boundaries with prejudiced people and communicate your expectations for how you should be treated.

Call out prejudiced behaviour: If you witness prejudiced behaviour, call it out and challenge the individual to examine their attitudes and beliefs.

Surround yourself with diversity: Surround yourself with a diverse group of individuals who are accepting and supportive.

Educate yourself and others: Educate yourself and others about the harmful effects of prejudice and work to promote understanding and acceptance.

Ultimately, avoiding prejudiced people may involve making difficult decisions about your relationships or situations. It's important to remember that you deserve to be surrounded by people who are accepting and supportive and that you have the power to set boundaries and protect yourself from harmful behaviour.

NARCISSIST

Narcissistic people are individuals who have an inflated sense of self-importance and a deep need for admiration and attention from others. They may have a lack of empathy for others and often manipulate or exploit those around them to meet their own needs. Narcissism is considered a personality disorder and can significantly impact a person's ability to form healthy relationships and function in society.

How to Recognize Narcissistic People:

Recognizing narcissistic people can be challenging, as they may initially come across as charming or charismatic. However, there are some signs to look for, such as:

Lack of empathy: Narcissistic people may have little concern for the feelings or needs of those around them.

Need for admiration: They may have a deep need for attention and admiration from others, often going to great lengths to receive praise or admiration.

Manipulative behaviour: Narcissistic people may manipulate or exploit others to meet their own needs, often without regard for the impact on others.

Grandiosity: They may have an exaggerated sense of self-importance and believe that they are superior to others.

How to Avoid Narcissistic People:

Avoiding narcissistic people can be challenging, as they may be a part of your social circle or workplace. However, there are some strategies that you can use to limit their impact on your life, such as:

Set boundaries: Set clear boundaries with narcissistic people and communicate your expectations for how you should be treated.

Be cautious: Be cautious when dealing with new people and take the time to get to know them before investing emotionally.

Seek support: Seek support from trusted friends, family members, or a therapist if you are struggling to navigate a relationship with a narcissistic person.

Practice self-care: Practice self-care and prioritize your own well-being when dealing with narcissistic people.

Ultimately, avoiding narcissistic people may involve making difficult decisions about your relationships or situations. It's important to remember that you deserve to be surrounded by people who are healthy and supportive and that you have the power to protect yourself from harmful behaviour.

FINAL THOUGHTS

T hroughout this book, we have explored the various masks that people wear and the negative behaviours that can be associated with them. From unfaithful and manipulative individuals to narcissistic and abusive people, these negative traits can impact our ability to form healthy relationships and lead fulfilling lives. However, it is important to remember that not all people fall into these categories, and building healthy relationships is still possible.

So let's explore some key principles for building healthy relationships and protecting ourselves from the negative impact of these negative behaviours. While we cannot control the behaviour of others, we can control our own actions and make choices that promote healthy relationships and positive interactions with those around us.

Communicate openly and honestly: Open and honest communication is the foundation of any healthy relationship. It is important to express your feelings, needs, and boundaries clearly and respectfully, while also being willing to listen to others and respect their perspectives.

Set clear boundaries: Setting clear boundaries is an important part of protecting yourself from negative behaviour. Be clear about your limits and communicate them clearly to others. If someone crosses a boundary, be willing to assert yourself and stand up for yourself.

Practice self-care: Practicing self-care is important for maintaining your own emotional and physical well-being. This can include activities like exercise, mindfulness, and spending time with loved ones.

Seek support: If you are struggling to navigate a difficult relationship or deal with the impact of negative behaviour, seek support from trusted friends, family members, or a therapist. They can provide you with guidance, support, and a fresh perspective.

Cultivate empathy and compassion: While it is important to protect yourself from negative behaviour, it is also important to cultivate empathy and compassion for others. Recognize that everyone has their own struggles and challenges, and try to approach interactions with kindness and understanding.

I would like to conclude it by saying that Building healthy relationships is possible, even in the face of negative behaviour from others. By practising open communication, setting clear boundaries, practising self-care, seeking support, and cultivating empathy and compassion, we can protect ourselves and build positive, fulfilling relationships with those around us. Remember, you deserve to be surrounded by people who are healthy and supportive, and you have the power to protect yourself from negative behavior and build the relationships that you deserve.